T0156515

A Spiritual Road Map

A Spiritual Road Map

✦

Robert Hrebin

iUniverse, Inc.
New York   Bloomington

A Spiritual Road Map

The views expressed in this work are solely those of the author and do not necessarily reflect the views of the publisher, and the publisher hereby disclaims any responsibility for them.

iUniverse books may be ordered through booksellers or by contacting:

iUniverse
1663 Liberty Drive
Bloomington, IN 47403
www.iuniverse.com
1-800-Authors (1-800-288-4677)

Because of the dynamic nature of the Internet, any Web addresses or links contained in this book may have changed since publication and may no longer be valid.

ISBN: 978-1-4401-8081-1 (sc)
ISBN: 978-1-4401-8080-4 (ebk)

Printed in the United States of America

iUniverse rev. date: 1/6/2010

Contents (SUMMARY)

Preface

An Introduction to Your Journey

This book is a study of God's designs that we know as virtue. This as a written study was not intended to teach you what you should believe in or how to believe in what you are. It was written solely to bring out who you are—as well as the best of who you are. It was written not to give answers but draw attention, peak curiosity and interest in the disciplines of life.

So here are some keys with directions for their use with your meditation exercises to help you maintain a free and open mind. Your free will is a virtue and as all virtues, they are immutable by Gods design and cannot be changed or altered by anyone, except for your refusal to acknowledge and use them. Always remember God knows who you are and what you need, but you must be open in all ways to what you need.

All religions can only be created, grown, and developed in one place—and that one place is in God. The twelve chapters that are described with God's direction and intentions for us to grow and flourish are presented using these concepts of growth and direction of growth while in meditation and prayer by using God's design of virtue for morality as guides of daily living in all matters.

Before you take a journey in these chapters, ask yourself if your interest in reading this leans toward the spiritual, quality-of-living or being a patriot for an ideal or organization or country.

Keep this question in mind as you read and explore. Maintain this order while visualizing and contemplating God, mind/soul/consciousness/ family and the structure to support all of this—whether it is nature or society or a combination of both. Be sure to leave your baggage at the beginning of each chapter.

A Spiritual Road Map

Every action and thought to man's inquiry of living becomes a spiritual presence in God with one distinction; that it is required to be established within the scheme of things, as a correct or incorrect use of these thoughts. There is an ever-diminishing spiral of upward spiritual travel, where the road becomes increasingly narrow as we climb it. These twelve letters are descriptions and suggestions on how to ask a question, so God knows the morality of your will and needs.

The spiritual definition in this book is that everything relating to a greater plane of awareness in nature, talent, and relationships, creates awareness in planes of our being. Man is a spiritual being using talent and intellectual expression. This allows him to know the day or night of life. Our experiences permit us to understand the design of the cosmos. The rhythm of the cosmos develops as morality is used and begins to demonstrate itself to us in all aspects of society as beauty. This then teaches us proportion in relationship to everything in the known cosmos. This is how we learn and grow by using practical experiences along with meditation life styles.

The Road's Name Is Talent

Talent is the expression of accumulated experiences that are not of any particular time or awareness of our being. The road's direction and meaning is our debut with God and all that is of God.

The Direction of Travel

Our mastery of self becomes an unending expansion of design. This book explores the cosmic engine known as "the amulet." It was forged by God's cosmic design. Its purpose is to display the many paths available to us. It is also used in life as roadways to be traveled for spiritual growth and assistance.

The descriptions that are put on paper in all of these letters are those reflections. In the following pages, you will not find answers to your questions—you will only find directions to find what you need to know for a happy and fruitful life.

Belief and Understanding of a Journey

Since spiritual being goes beyond your understanding, it becomes a religious statement to be looked up to with humility and determination to grow. If understanding is allowed to be your experience, it then becomes moral action in every spiritual sense. It reflects off of virtue as a beacon in the night and gives us added understanding.

Our Fuel for Traveling

We are creative, imaginative, and independent beings requiring pictures for the mind and soul to explore. These attributes are given fuel in allegories, fables, fairy tales, and other stories. Our inquisitive natures and our need to express ourselves socially cause us to always use one interpretation of this tool—when controversy develops another interpretation will develop out of the controversy creating new fuel to travel spiritually.

Soul's Engine

The soul has polarities of a sort—or as we understand—polarities of positive and negative. The positive is action or the builder. This part will ensure that its contract made before the first breath of birth will be completed before taking the last breath of transition. It is the building direction of the mind and soul that will experience hell and high water in order to complete the contract. The negative is the giver—the protector, the nurse, and the doctor that are always embracing us to assure our arrival at our destination.

Engine Repair

The rebalancing, redirecting, and dispelling of myths and superstitions become the responsibility of science. Its disciplines include philosophy, engineering, physics, theoretical mathematical expressions, history, anthropology, and religious studies. This permits the growth of all animate structures—from one person to groups of people in international and global societies. This is the design and sequence of events that we are bound to through God's creation.

Examples for Today's Challenges

Darwin's theory of evolution cannot be believed, because belief is religious and goes beyond nature. However, it can be understood as a scientific presentation of nature that adds to a greater understanding of the cosmos and God's laws of creation.

Reincarnation cannot be believed because its spiritual meaning can only be demonstrated between you and God as a direction of spiritual growth. This becomes a very personal experience and is difficult for social interpretation—allowing a presentation of language and mind pictures that we must learn in this life can be difficult if not impossible to express as God intended us to understand from our inner experiences.

Growth

Awareness of the third dimension of varying formats and degrees of them become instruction to elevate spiritual awareness. This is like a coin tossed into the ocean—keeping in mind the size of the coin to the unending appearance of the ocean—and the ocean is less than the power and strength of your soul. However, our awareness unlike the coin can be a limiting factor of ignorance and social practices that prevent a spiritual sense of direction within the unending power of the soul.

These unexplored directions are what we need to learn. These directions are what we need to complete as our agreed-upon contracts that were made before we took our first breaths.

The purpose of this life is to learn about virtue as spiritual presentation in its purest forms—not our social interpretation that belongs to a lesser form of expression.

Spiritual exploration must remain infinitely open to mind and perception of thought.

If we are to grow spiritually, there can be no limitations set by the suggestions and examples of life experiences. There can only be the willingness to explore new spiritual roads.

Continue the Journey

Occasionally, we may reflect our present and new accumulations of life on life's terms and then tomorrow we must set our sails and compasses for our continuing journey. Darwin's theory and reincarnation can be a limitation to this journey. Take nothing with you except for your need to know—with no restrictions of yesterday to slow you down.

This statement is for the innocent at heart—not the expert of social expression. The traveler's cart is loaded down with all the possessions that might be needed for the journey. They will never be needed—only the cumbersome weight of his required effort will be felt.

Freedom must always be where we can go with God's blessings—as nomads in the desert going from one oasis to another or explorers on the seas going from port to port.

Addictions of the Road

Be careful what you wish for. In order to be creative in his expression of his art form, the artist travels a road that must be continuously traveled. The individuals that use this road do not have a problem when on it—only when they are not. The need to be on this road can be overwhelming. It sets up the need to be on it at all times. Many times, drugs show a path to this road that is not lasting in creativity. It is destructive in life and an addiction is born. There are those who have the discipline and spiritual presence to circumvent this dilemma and are patient enough to find the road as sober and willing disciples. There are many other roads that are not as obvious, but can be just as addicting.

Look For Opportunities

May we become full of our passions for living in our dreams and journeys and never regret a passed or missed opportunity. The goal ultimately is to have an equal balance of both in the makeup of our personality for its growth and development.

When "things go bump in the night," settle yourself and look for a new road brought to your attention by this intrusion into your tranquility. As a guide when using the absolutes as a spiritual aid, do not substitute:

- Low self-esteem for love,
- Pride for purity,
- Ruthlessness for selflessness, or
- Intolerance for honesty.

These mindsets are defects of character—unlike the absolutes. The only outcome that always develops from this use is fear to one degree or another—not spiritual freedom.

Join me in exploring the twelve facets of the jewel known as the cosmos. The twelve letters in this manuscript—not unlike the twelve components of the amulet—are complete only with the awareness, imagination, talent, and desire needed to explore them.

Yours truly,
Robert Hrebin

Introduction

Quantum—
All Potential Is Undefined Energy

As we all experience with our minds, we look into what we assume to be emptiness. We have an ever-present need for something identifiable to mind and consciousness for acknowledgement within itself. If there is a lack of response, we assume that there is nothing there. However, so-called nothing must be something because we are conscious of it. It is simply a label that consciousness places on the experience that would appear to be void of anything familiar. We are always looking for something different or unfamiliar to explore. Is potential the need that society creates or is potential the timeliness of the great design of the mind of God?

Patents and major discoveries are good examples of growth rather than random chance discovery. There has never been a recorded history of events where only one person or institution has been working on a major discovery that may have led to patents without someone or some other institution working on the same thing in closely guarded secrecy. This statement challenges the assumption of the unique and original idea. We can never think beyond what God is, nor less then what God is. So to say that God is everything is the challenge to the original idea. Keeping this in mind, some inventor may have had the same idea; but was not the first to claim it as his or maybe just to complete it to make a model type for presentation. In either case, potential develops into consciousness as we require it from necessity or as we grow. This certainly is not absolute proof of this statement, but patent offices, layers and historians have proven this many times over. In addition, if this is a correct statement, then what have we not yet discovered—or what have we not yet become—as spiritual people and societies that would lead us to new and greater discoveries possibly with new sciences.

If we acknowledge that nothing is something, then something must be potential. Only minds can use this potential energy by acting upon it in an assertive manor. All potential-is undefined energy and undefined energy cannot be mathematically proven without a model that already exists. Geometry symbols are the controlling factor that permits a definition in the consciousness of measurable existence. Refer to model (a) The Amulet on page XX.

Origin Is Not Mathematically Provable

Origin is a one-dimensional starting plane for convergence of sorts. Its focal point is an intersecting point or points that appear to be random. Its reflective action against its ever-expanding outer boundary makes the second dimension. This reflective beginning will eventually cover all minute segments of degrees in both longitude and latitude within this sphere in cycles.

This is what mathematics must follow when potential becomes two-dimensional by mind acting on origin. Mathematics was given to us to use in display and to describe the expression of proportion. With the use of mathematics in science it helps dispel personal opinion and superstition.

Origin becomes part of the reflection within the sphere as the beginning manifestation that we call positive and negative in all relationships. Eastern philosophy calls it yin and yang or simply two opposing forces. In mathematics, this would be defined as odd and even numbers.

1. One = origin—which is not provable with mathematics because it is potential. Potential is the only way to describe infinity. From this potential develops design and structure of creation.

2. Two = the sphere drawn as a circle permits reflection of origin against itself. This reflection becomes conscious design that is what we know as virtue and virtue is all things. When this is permitted to develop more completely beyond reflection, it then becomes conscious.

3. One and two are the beginning of our numerical system and our beginning understanding of proportion, which is what we know as mathematics from which all other numbers evolve and are used.

4. One impacted with two = three, etc. To infinity. Further examples would be: $3+1=4$, $3+2=5$, $3+3=6$, $6+5=11$, $1+11=12$; this because of the established reflection of God will become a random mixing of numbers that we come to know as proportion, which is then displayed to us as scientific law of infinity that we understand as God's creation.

What does this demonstrate as a model? It demonstrates that our minds created all of what we are and what we experience as free personalities in God's design of creation. All of what we experience and are exposed to develops each mind as a free expression of the whole existence of everything; this takes us to our beliefs in our religions and philosophies.

The brain must then be an expression of mind and imagination—a function of mind with all of its attributes of talent and memory. Mind must learn to express itself within the demonstrations set by nature—as the laws of science are slowly developed to reflect the action of creation. Mind is a part of the infinite—with unlimited potential of all things—but it cannot freely participate as this free unlimited agent without proving its free, parallel, and unobstructed association of infinite design as a co-partnership of virtue.

Let me explore this symbol and it's components that represent all things in creation. This symbol represents the very smallest part of creation called the microcosm, to the very largest part of creation called the macrocosm.

1. Number 1 represents origin, which is shown as a point.
2. Number 2 represents the sphere, which is shown as a circle that the mind of God established to reflect with in origin and the sphere, this to our understanding creates design of virtue and the potential of all living things within this design.
3. Numbers 3- 6 represents a base from which all things are a design of proportion within virtue, within these parameters of virtue become guides in positive supportive thought as well as third dimension creation – east, west, north, south; earth, wind, fire, water; love, selflessness, honesty, purity; etc.
4. Numbers 7–12 represent the reflections of potential acted upon by mind - their geometric symbols are the equal lateral triangle. The triangle with its point facing up is mans attempt to communicate with God, which is defined as finite communication. The triangle with its point facing down is Gods attempt to communicate with man, which is defined as infinite communication. There will be more disclosed on all of these geometric functions in the following chapters.
5. All other line set combinations are, variations of these four groups of geometric designs. They are mans attempt to more completely understand virtue in

a more comprehensive way. All this is mathematics expressing virtue in its purist form called proportion.

For mind, the ability to manifest thought and the realization of thought in a balanced and useful format is essential to support all of these design expressions from above explanations 1- 4 using his free will.

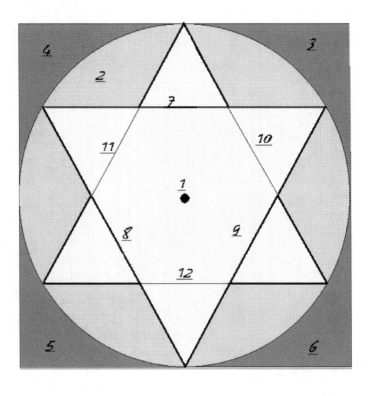

To further explore what the square can represent, I will give some graphic examples concerning balance of design. Science treats symptoms of illnesses and tries to assist the patient into regaining their energy balance before any permanent injuries take place. Before any such condition can—or will—take place, there is a proper lifestyle. If it is practiced, it may prevent illnesses that have psychosomatic beginnings. This is not to suggest that traditional medicine and treatments should be ignored if illness occurs. This is only to suggest that if proper living were engaged in—then illness may not occur. This lifestyle is absent in what is referred to as the seven deadly sins.

One of the best examples is the Indian musical instrument called the sitar. It is a string instrument with two sets of strings. The first string is the music string and the string next to it is sympathetic in its very design. This string only vibrates with the musical string next to it is struck. This string was designed and used similar to the nervous system of all animated life—it has a sympathetic nervous system that science is just beginning to explore and investigate. This implies that the musician is responsible for the state of his own energy. As he strikes his own chords of life, he can bring himself into or out of balance or harmony with the design of both micro and macrocosm.

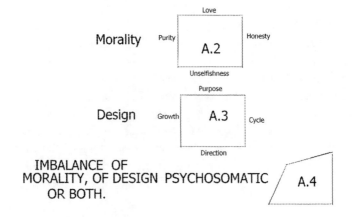

What this represents is the inability to take advantage of the true design as it was conceived—and the true design is capable of infinite power. Some lifestyles and thought habits can cause this problem and limit power. The seven deadly sins are:

1. Lust
2. Gluttony
3. Greed
4. Sloth
5. Wrath
6. Envy
7. Pride

There are two conditions that can help complicate recognizing these sins and they are:

Incorrect scientific principles
Genetic cultural inheritances

So, beware that they do not cloud your perception of these seven sins.

The mind's action on all potential permits consciousness as we know and understand it, but we must first define what potential is. Otherwise it is only chaos, which does not fit the initial design.

The mystics say going from one plane of consciousness to another can make some attributes of mind unnecessary—some of my brief experiences have confirmed how this might be possible. As I understand these experiences and attempt to describe them, find myself having difficulty expressing them and also begin to realize we are becoming the very thing that we are trying to define and describe.

Chapter 1

Random Thoughts and Understanding of Them

✦

Upon awakening one morning, I was left with a lingering image or vision of an unlimited creative plane. There was a spectrum of creativity that represented everything that is the cosmos and beyond. The spectrum emanating from this plane was an oasis in the desert. It is our sustenance for our journey called life. The five senses are within this spectrum and the spectrum is beyond their capabilities in all directions imagined. This creates awareness on our journey; the oasis was referred to as sin (everything measurable).

Our Direction Called Home

This spectrum of energies was also the covenant that God made with man; it appeared as a rainbow in a biblical allegory. The energy was not compatible with its source. The intended design created an insoluble mix like oil and water. This created the dilemma in all of us—we must be ready to leave one to become a part of the other. This is also called "the twelfth hour."

This is the direction of our real home—the place where the soul and its personality wish to reside. However, our consciousness at birth affords us the opportunity to express who we are as free agents within the image of God with the limits of the measurable.

Like children, we are apprehensive about leaving those things that we created and surround self. Whatever we have created in us is ours and ours alone. The spiritual axiom called "the hole in the donut" asks what will become of us if we abandon ourselves in our present lifestyle of thinking and social interaction.

Therefore, more often than not, we are overly concerned about the missing "us"—and not so elated over the brave new world that we will encounter and enjoy one day-on our journey.

A Study for the Heart's Intended Perfection

Due to its simplicity, a candle makes a worthy and compelling subject. Picture a candle with an elegant, tapered body. The length complements the taper and diameter, drawing attention to itself as an object of perfect proportion. Often, things of perfect proportion do not require any supporting background to be noticed and admired; they are the formula for completion of proportion.

The farther that we stray from this so-called perfect design, the more it becomes apparent that supporting backgrounds and complementary furnishings become a necessary part to help display this candle in its own right as part of a proportionate display, to be as pleasing to an admirers eye as the candle of perfect proportion.

Picture the different possibilities of design for this very simple instrument of light: short, wide, tall, various colors, all kinds of inscribed designs with relief, and many carved forms. However, its sole purpose is to create light where light is required. It has one important principle to demonstrate—the visible and elegant demonstration of transferring energy from one state of existence to another. As the flame burns and melts the wax, the candle is slowly used up and loses its mass ending its performance.

Unattainable Perfection

To discover the elegance by which all virtuous things conduct and redirect their energies within their life cycles of our awareness is the most beautiful and caring experience that can be given to this process—especially on animated creations throughout the cosmos.

This is the beginning of understanding higher principles of creation and understanding the importance of all objects, as they may appear to us on first glance and then with greater familiarity later on. Then there is more attention that is placed on how the energy flow and redirection of these energies complements its presentation as the cosmos has designed. Therefore, the redirection of these energies in all animate objects is a work in progress—not a completed expression.

Objectivity of Useful Plans

The realization is that there is a correct way to use this sin and maintain the objectivity that is displayed with the example of the candle. We are totally within our rights as free and growing agents—or entities of the cosmos—to use sin to develop and grow beyond the available spiritual plains.

Is there an incorrect way to use sin and lose our objectivity? The answer must be yes.

The wrong use of sin would be if everything to be gained from a particular aspect of sin were complete within ourselves—and no one else could benefit from it in the form that we are using it and we refuse to release it—it may set up a dilemma that we may not become free by ourselves.

This sets up the possibility that this energy can spill over into our imaginations. In addition, since all original purpose has been satisfied, the spectrum of sin has no real or needed purpose. It runs the risk of becoming perverted within the unlimited and possibly uncontrolled planes of our imagination.

To Be the Gardener

We are given humility and ego—each tool with its own design and purpose—to build and tend our gardens of the mind and soul. We have great trees of knowledge and bushes that create boundaries to prevent unwanted weeds from outside to overtake the flower garden of our labor and design. Like the thoughts in these chapters, they must be free with the pictures and directions of the mind—not the weeds of discord.

Humility is the gentle breeze of knowledge and the sun radiating through the gentle raindrops of the day. It provides all that is needed for your garden to take sustenance from the power and strengths that ego can provide. Ego—as a force used correctly with imagination, talent, and intellect—can move mountains. Alternatively, it can turn up the refuse in your garden that has fallen from weeds and replant the many seeds of despair and ignorance.

Continuous Growth

Remember that our gardens are made up from one's own imagination—as well as ongoing experiences that become the sum total of our experiences, including everything in all of our reincarnations that has been recorded and stored in the permanent (mystical) records of God.

This is the reason why a healthy and spiritual lifestyle is paramount to our spiritual growth and unlimited freedom as a free and creative being of the cosmos.

To continue briefly on reincarnation, let us understand the comparison of the theory of Darwin's selective evolution that science has explored and brought to light. It is a process by which nature endorses to establish a more complete and durable expression of animation. Reincarnation is simply the same process on a different plane.

Infinite Love

Our expression of infinite love is the formula of the sphere. It is usually shown as a circle with a center dot. The process that creates awareness for us to enjoy and use is the center radiating to its reflective boundaries. It is no more a lifestyle than selective evolution—it is a process that requires that we radiate from our nucleus to the limits of who we are in the privacy of self. This allows us to know our true natures on all levels of awareness and what we need to improve and become. The true love of God always forgives and is always willing to assist our requests and needs, when help is requested on specific needs or problems.

To make any more of this can lead to the incorrect use of imagination. Here are some timeless sayings that support the contents of this letter. "My cup is overflowing"—but what will the overflow randomly mix with and possibly reanimate in the hold of your ship?

The timeless saying known almost universally "Mystic, know thyself"— simply translates to taking all opportunities to know yourself in meditation and development of our interests of God given talent. The more you are familiar with self, the greater freedom you will enjoy in all things.

Another saying "Practice moderation in all things"— translates to balance is our responsibility and becomes our experienced delight in daily affairs. Slowly, we will become compatible with our soul and its attributes. We will become trustworthy in all things encountered. We will be allowed to stay and develop as a complete entity—growing and developing as one with the cosmos and mastering all that we are.

Chapter 2

The Gift with Our Best Intentions

✦

A spiritual gift has its beginning where the mystical and the moral are all one with the heart. The heart points to the direction that the mind and soul will explore.

A gift, which will have its greatest meaning as something given on special occasions or to recall special memories of past events, must include the direction given by the heart. A gift from a friend can become a gesture of a very special relationship. It can also be something that the recipient might never acquire for themselves because of financial limitations, availability, or feelings of worth in their station of social standing. A gift can give value and great significance to a friendship. These gifts are certainly important to a happy social life, but will be of a leaser gift, if not for the hearts direction. The heart becomes the driving force to a more complete meaning of the gift and more completely displays the true meaning from the giver.

The Strengths of Humility

The heart will attempt to direct your intentions, but may be silent at times. We may not be aware of our presentation or whether the recipient would even welcome it. If we are sure that our motives are correct, sometimes your presence or example may be all that is needed to present a gift from within.

The Greater Gifts

However, what about the gifts that you receive from God before retiring to sleep or in a moment of relaxation?

It will be your decision to explore and become these experiences. The jewel of the cosmos, the domain of virtue, and the spiritual jewelry will eventually adorn your personality. Be patient and accepting of these things, they will grow in you—if care is taken by the gardener in your garden to allow them to bloom.

Giving Is Spiritual Growth

Our need to give is driven by our need to grow spiritually; this is part of the basic design and cannot be altered. Here is where the heart must speak in tones of God. If it does not come from the design of God, it is not virtuous and is of little value.

Growth through Free Will

In order to accept or recognize less then what has been anticipated with an act of giving, the heart must remind you of true needs of growth. If not it will leave only fear—an illusion brought on by ignorance that is mistaken for virtue.

The heart reminds us of our needed direction and always takes great care not to interfere with our free will if we should go a different way. We then demonstrate that we are still not aware enough to provide a needed course correction so that our ship can sail in the direction of freedom. As captains of our ship, we have once again failed.

As a virtuous thought and deed are freely given and if its energy is rejected, the remainder of its energy as a gift will diminish. Once stopped, it may never be completed as a gem of God's virtue with its many facets of expression. It will only become fragmented like the petals of a dry, dying rose.

Rewards of Kindness and Patience

These rejections may only be a temporary set back because infinity has no end and love is infinite. If a dying rosebud can be reborn as a new flower—as nature demonstrates day by day—Then know for certain that your gift remains with God as your request by prayer until one day there is a request for this gift by your intended recipient.

The Teacher

For it is not enough to take a stand and say that God wills it. In truth, it would be enough to say that I will it and I am a student of God. So let the one who accepts my gift teach me—for I am only a student as well.

We are not doormats to be used by others with uncaring, callous, or cruel acts performed in the name of something greater than them selves. It is their choice for their benefit—for the illusion of their own shortcomings or defects of character. They may display these traits as honorable, but they fall short of the pure, loving act of a true gift.

There are random opportunities throughout our lives to meet and know one another, as husband and wife or a friendship of more than casual importance to us. Opposites attract—not as good and evil—but with personality attributes and qualities. Which is what each one of us is or is not on a spiritual and personal makeup to others in all of our social experiences.

Even though these can be powerful attractions, there are social and gender conditions that can limit them. The limitations are imposed by the current need of a personality. When accepting an experience, the most pleasant and meaningful outcome is always our intention and expectation. Sometimes this is not possible and I feel sad for those who do not have a choice. If it is your karma, learn it quickly so it will end and seek help from others to support your new direction.

Spiritual Growth

Giving a gift is in the best understanding of God. The energy left with them to allow growth will be returned at one hundred times its figurative strength to you in the way of spiritual strength and awareness. However, make no mistake that this is not your doing—it is designed into creation. (See Ref. 2.3.)

Time as we know it is not a part of this simple formula. The infinite does not measure time limited to the mundane. The mundane is a form of animation that will explode as the seasons do as an awakening from a sleep or the excitement that a child displays with something that is entertaining being presented to it or the fireworks on the Fourth of July. (See Ref. 2.2.)

Use the stability of the square and ask questions using the formula of the triangle as the gate to higher illumination of the cosmos. You will leave little for less worthy thoughts to develop within your meditations and consciousness. This develops into great pleasure and joy following this path. (See Ref. 11.1.)

Our growth will develop by focusing our minds and allowing our talents to develop in many directions. The adversity of these experiences will serve to strengthen our character and personality. When the Japanese manufacture their steel swords, they reheat and fold the raw material many times to build into the steel a cross-grain structure that is superior in strength. This is not usually accepted as pleasurable in many experiences—except for the results that it often produces later on in life.

This will prevent you from placing great value on only one aspect of virtue and forcing it to become an extreme experience at best, if not a great disappointment. Think about expressing your self through spiritual overtones in gifts, such as art, music, painting, sculpture, or poetry.

Then contemplate the opportunities that are waiting for you that may go beyond your meager inspirations of thought and talent to something grand and exciting.

Here are some suggestions on how to meditate on these letters—if you have not done so already.

Group 1: Chapters #8-the promise, #12-the absolutes, and #6-freedom. Group-1 is layout on (Triangle 2.1). Group-2 & 3 can be used the same way or other examples that you may want to tryout in this way.

Group 2: Chapters #7-adversity, #4-the image of God, and #10-the journey.

Group 3: Chapters #1-random thoughts, #3-the virtue of simplicity, and #9the language of the heart

Now take these letters in total freedom of who you are and what you understand from your perspective. I was promised that there will-be help on your journey. Do not settle for almost in anything or a second best in understanding and joy.

A Spiritual Road Map

Two triangles assembled one on top of the other (2.3)

Chapter 3

The Simplicity of Virtue

✦

Plato said, "Virtue is everything that is good." Christ demonstrated the simplicity of virtue.

Establishing and using a mindset of concentration serves as a meditative state of exploration.

When an answer is given through this awareness, it is sometimes shown as a complete picture of the entire subject presented at once. This gives the appearance of a dynamic, vibrant presentation instead of what we are accustomed to know as an intellectual experience.

It becomes a mental image to convey a meaning and direction of thought concerning all aspects of the question asked. As a precious gem with many facets, it stands alone. This becomes your responsibility as a free member of the cosmos to express this experience—using words and other forms of communication called talent. So, then conversation is the alternative form of meditation experience, with effort on the part of God being directed to you.

A meditation experience of vibrant dynamic energy or what is called a living word cannot replace one's own experience; only facets of this meditation can be described at any one time. While a person's experience of real life encounters that may have a similar experience in its message as a meditation experience, will become very clear as an intellectual experience because of the support of our five senses. The two of these experiences put together become even more dynamic then as separate experiences. While a person's experience of real life encounters that may be similar to a meditation experience in message become very clear. So, then conversation is the alternative form of meditation experience, with effort on the part of God being directed to you. Either way they both are a meditation experience. The first experience described is of another plane of consciousness, while the last one is on our plane of consciousness that we now reside on.

If I present the following statements as allegory, they will better fit our everyday relationships—especially when concerning ourselves with nothing more than daily living. This permits acceptance, which is the first step to learning all things. The explanation of all virtue must encompass who we are within the relationship of the cosmos.

The Gem as an Attraction

As with the gem and its many facets, each facet is a distinct part with unique color and imperfections. This observation is closer to its uniqueness that makes it what it is from its raw and uncontrolled form. If it were magnified, we could see the facets in greater detail—until the magnification becomes so great that only the atomic structure is visible, this is its construction as in all things that are mundane. We make the raw material so that its natural beauty is displayed and enhanced as something unique, by using our talents and imagination as guides of grace and beauty.

The Conductor of a Thought

Another example is the use of color. Three colors—yellow, blue, and red—create endless combinations of all other colors. As their energies combine, they make these infinite variations—just as three notes can make endless melodies.

The word gem is used to better identify the experiences of our meditations. Take away the physical aspects of these models and use only what is left. What is left will be your own reflection of thought traveling through you. It will add to your own uniqueness and create what will become one of the songs of your life.

The Orchestra Is a Tool to Explore Your Songs

The orchestra can develop cosmic algorithms with the awareness of our needs. This will always create an inner melody of thought to the scheme of all things that we will use to develop within the design of the cosmos.

They can then be used to play a new song of science or the arts with the five senses acting as instruments in an orchestra. There are three facets of virtue that can become receptacles or guides to embrace and excite the five senses. The facets and color—like those of the gem—are good representatives of our soul. We do not know the makeup of their talent or permanent memory—or even what they are in the grand scheme of things. They are similar to the polished gem—complete freestanding items that relate to the soul.

When we are receptive to understanding God's virtue, our dreams and aspirations are illuminated with virtue. Just as a light illuminates a gem, we are permitted to explore our inner selves more completely. We can also see or experience what we are becoming and working to become. Our direction and intended form opens like a rose from a bud to a flower. Our awareness grows and opens in similar ways.

Become the Colors and Notes That We Show and Sing

To more completely embrace the directions that talent, permanent memory, and awareness are capable of empowering, use the various symbols of communication and their designed functions as described in the letter called "quantum." How many different roses are there? One more fitting to our personality than another and then the color complements as well as the type of rose showing off our personality as a painting does its frame.

Symphony—Variations of Your Song to Be Sung

If you hold a color sample that is identical to a color on your wall at home, it becomes difficult—if not impossible—to see these colors as two separate color palettes. The contrasts are not distinct because they are parallel in hue of the basic color. We also encounter this condition within our inner selves.

Talent, permanent memory, and awareness have developed with our efforts. Potential can go beyond anything we can perceive today. Because we have discovered new roads through our efforts of sharing our songs with others, a design develops that will permit a new symphony to appear. Suddenly, "our weaknesses may become our strengths, and our so-called strengths may become our weaknesses." Whoever wrote this quote understood the principles of the contrasting color palettes.

Energies form a new gem that will become the experiences and adventures of the mind. It will direct and illuminate your story as a new song of the heart—the song that you and you alone can create from talent, permanent memory, and awareness.

The Song Is an Endless Cycle of Improvement

Tomorrow is always a new beginning—a new day in a spiritual way of referring to a day that you think may be nearing completion. This will show itself as a self-professed weakness that one-day makes itself known as a visible and uplifting strength. However, there must be spiritual presence of mind to support its true attributes of thought for this to emerge as strength. For what would appear to be lacking in development may be a parallel co-existence with God's virtues. There is no visible contrast between them—just as the colors on the wall try to explain.

Comedy and Tragedy

Beware of the bridge that spans loneliness and despair from our soul to our awareness of self. Intellect can describe it, but cannot become this bridge because intellect is a tool. The greater the void, the greater the need to traverse it with something to lessen the spiritual pain it creates. In order to make a bridge, intellect and ego will collaborate. Out of this collaboration, an addiction will be born and its intended use is to lessen the spiritual pain of the victim.

To eliminate this addiction, there will be a seed that uses raw materials from the garden called soul. This garden with its seeds in bloom; create the building materials needed for attributes, such as willingness and free will. It uses them to construct an indestructible foundation to fill these voids and forever eliminate spiritual pain.

The Garden Called Soul

All variations of energy that we plant in our garden form an awareness that may become our music in ways similar to a symphony. We share this symphony with those who will listen. The more balanced our approach to these variations of energy that have been planted, the more beautiful and balanced our symphony will be. The more we embrace the cosmic with our melody, the more we entertain those who listen. The only thing that we can do is be-true to ourselves, suggesting that our thoughts must be parallel to our true natures. Religion and society guide our efforts to express who we are for the sake of others.

Virtue will become its own song with inspirations of self. Guided by these rules, it will become a symphony with many variations. Spiritual is everything cosmic—and this is what we strive to express—it has little to do with the labels that we may place on them. Being all that one can be does not require an education—only an avenue to express and to explore. Education will extend our expressions. Some of us do better than others do—not because society approves or disapproves, but through the peace that radiates from within. This is the simplicity of virtue in its most complete form.

Taking Care of the Garden

The reason to be very selective and think carefully is to be moral. It perfects our balance. It is the means to an end of total freedom. The beauty of the garden is in its display as free agents of the cosmos.

Simple geometric shapes remind us of proportion. And the many cycles of practice become the rhythm of our song. The rhythm repeats as cycles to support the symphony—whether it is complex or simple. The rhythm may change within the symphony, but the cycles repeat and improve. This is the direction of the cosmic.

This is the true design of God that permits us to become more aware of the cosmos and its full spectrum as a unique understanding, without limitations or controls of our dreams or aspirations sung by talent, memory, and awareness.

Thoughts to Be Careful Of

One thing that should be understood is that we cannot become evil using infinite creativity as its source of power. Only the illusions of an evil thought that we trap within our consciousness permit the use of this illusion. Here we would be in total control and yet dominant only within our own ignorance and self-imposed limitations that we call freedom.

The Variations of Imbalance

The principle of color verses contrast is compared to strengths versus weaknesses. Very often, children and their parents have similar dispositions and physical appearances, but their interests and talents are entirely different. This is not always the case, but it happens often enough that it could not be just a random coincidence. Permanent memory, talent, and awareness of mind would be the true guiding forces and not genetics. Parenting would then be responsible for the balance within the child instead of the child's talents.

Keeping this in mind, use the triangle and the square for direction and understanding. Remember that they are formulas for all spiritual travelers and all formulas used correctly work as they are designed to. This makes the unfamiliar familiar and allows the lost to rediscover the correct highway to their destination.

Establish these formulas in your mind during your meditative moments—especially those new uncharted adventures that you may occasionally undertake. Remember that good habits might take a little longer to establish, while bad ones were established with seemingly little effort. They were most likely established using highly visible weaknesses of our ignorance that were interpreted as being true strengths. We are all subject to the incorrect use of our limitations that our awareness will present to us from time to time.

Therefore, to know virtue in its simplest and purest form, we must become it—or as the saying "progress not perfection" is the order—in all things that we encounter. Both animate and inanimate subject matter are both from the realm of God and subject to the same laws and virtue. Substitute the three attributes of mind-thought, action, and cycle with conductor, orchestra, and symphony:

- Thought=conductor
- Action=orchestra
- Cycle=symphony.

Remember that thought, action, cycle are playgrounds for meditation. They are your raw materials to work with and display as you see fit, so enjoy.

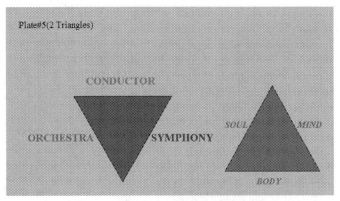

Two separate triangles
(3.1 labeled conductor, orchestra, and symphony)
(3.2 labeled soul, mind, and body)

Chapter 4

The Image of God As I Know It

✦

We are in the image of God, but cannot reflect against the image. We are blocked in our own universe of awareness and can only see our own lesser reflection. This is the price we must pay to learn independence of choice and action as was introduced to us within the cosmos. So how do we get to know God?

Man must grow into God. God invites man when an answer to a question can be given without interfering with man's freedom of thought or deed of positive intent—and learning that there are no exceptions in life to doing the correct thing.

Reflection As Infinity Directs

Learn to look beyond what you may think is the final answer compiled by your experiences. Ask a question about what you have done and what you are about to do? It may be a new spiritual adventure and this is your new starting point for another journey. You will see God in a more complete way.

Care must be taken for anything described verbally—so it does not become less than the meditated image. Care must also be taken so that your description does not simply become a reflection of yourself. There is nothing ventured of a new understanding or adventure if it is contaminated by well-meaning memories of self.

Friendship and Giving

To help you understand this statement, think of a true friendship with someone—a special relationship or a successful marriage. There are many things that we understand and accept about these relationships that are not necessarily what we would be as individuals. However, because of this relationship, we are willing to accept the total package. This is the unconditional acceptance that we must adopt when looking for an answer in meditation or in our sleep—anything less would interfere with the realm of God.

The Dangling Carrots of Life

The road to our spiritual journey narrows with respect to the mundane and widens with respect to the infinite. Virtue is God and it constantly simplifies and purifies our perception. The incentive is that the closer you get to the truth of God's new adventure for you, the greater the rush of energy that is unlike anything else you can experience.

With a pompous attitude, we display what we are sure that we know is in the interest of God. We hope that these ostentatious social directions of art, politics, business with all of its variations, belong to success or failure due to our efforts and not some karma that we cannot understand or control. We hope that these actions will somehow accomplish what the heart started by directing its display of talents. Somehow it will set a direction and will become the things that are virtuous. However, to do this, first ask the question.

The First Steps Taken To Learn Our Place

When we take our first breath, our awareness of order and principles of the mundane are equal to our spiritual understanding. However, with immaturity, there is limited ability to express this balance. Self, family, and community that are in balance and harmony must develop in use these two directions of awareness.

The struggles in our lives indicate an imbalance due to a lack of developed awareness to new spiritual directions and an undeveloped spiritual path. So then ask for directions. For complete and helpful experiences when meditating, they give us a very spiritual expression.

The circumstances born out of pomp become the facts that are the justified excuses for failure. This failure then becomes the fabric and direction of our next attempt to improve our actions, if we are careless in our thoughts to analyze our failures we will repeat the same failure. To make a point out of this experience, did your question become answered or did we simply over look the needed answer?

No matter how well our plans are displayed socially, they are driven by personal needs. Our professions, our chosen mates, and the social settings—do any of these situations fit into your question? This is all brought about by curiosity and our desire to know just how closely we parallel the image of God.

Crisis as the Director

We must acknowledge a new and all-consuming awareness within us—crisis. After all, everything has been initiated through our teacher—character. Our first breath activates our senses. Slowly our consciousness begins and causes us to compromise our contract with God with new promises of many exciting adventures.

It is also crisis that will by her very nature exist as a potential of strengths and weaknesses, before our first breaths are taken. Crisis will remind us that something is missing. For all that will go around, our agreement with God must come around to be completed. It is our covenant with God. Time has no restrictions or limitations in this relationship—except to imprison what has not yet been completed. This is the nature of crisis as virtue.

Crisis becomes first our spiritual pain and then our tour guide for this road. One day, it will be completed as agreed upon by you and God.

At times, we must question our usefulness, our spiritual growth, and awareness.

The Tools of Meditation and Experience

God is in us and we are in God. Every breath, every stone, every drop of water, and imagined thought becomes a unique oneness within God.

Therefore, we will compare love—as we understand it—with our character. Our unquenchable curiosity will be used as unselfishness. The emotion of crisis tries to develop itself into honesty. The circumstances of daily living cause all of our attempts to be pure in purpose. This becomes our foundation.

We need not lose the image of God because it is everything that we are and nothing if we reject it. However, to strengthen it is to grow more complete.

We explore two methods with blind obedience—meditation and firsthand experience. The first will be a gift from God's cosmos because of our request in prayer. The other is an experience of varied karmic teachings, initiated by life.

The image of God grows brighter and stronger with every effort. The tools that we have been given measure our daily lives in all of our senses and prayer. These tools permit us to question our success or failure and label them as moral or immoral life styles.

These tools help us to know our direction and destination of our oneness in life within nature; they are used as gyroscopes in great ships of the oceans.

To Close On What Is Learned

I started my spiritual nature to develop and express, just the same as countless others. I disliked the lifestyle and position that I found myself in. My instincts guided reason and critical decisions leading me to one conclusion—to leave this purgatory only after I had learned everything there was for me to know.

When boredom became the dominating emotion—instead of anger or confusion—then it would be time to move on. For I knew that the personality, thought processes, and potential talent were mine to cultivate under these conditions.

When the time came that I could see what was being developed as a result of my earlier efforts, there was an obvious strength of character and spiritual boldness. They were mine to keep and mine to forge new paths with success or failure—no matter what the instinctive master plan started out as.

If I had not taken this road, the confrontation with success or failure might have had a hollow ring to it. There would be no questions to ask and no new directions to explore. This reward was a freedom in awareness that covered all directions and colors of life—and it had started with my written experiences.

There were many times that I had viewed myself no better than the scavengers of the earth—there was little available to them in their domain that appeared attractive to me. However, isn't that what "beauty is in the eye of the beholder" means? I began to see how they flourish in their domain.

The Beauty of the Swan

When things go wrong, it can be beneficial to you—as a student of God—to keep it with you as a reminder. It is always desirable to be the swan and the partridge—but they may not be your lessons. Remember that the scavengers fill a noble purpose and thrive in nature. Continue to ask your questions.

This is my experience—I pray that you experience your own as completely as I did and that it complements you as the unique individual that you are.

Chapter 5

Meditation Is the Portal to "Quantum"

✦

A word, a thought, a phrase, or a picture gives me the direction to meditating. The game plan is to stay open, stay open, and stay open. Meditation is a way of realigning ourselves with the creative and supporting energies of the soul and its garden. With meditation, we may seek out new direction. We use trust and time to let us know—through the portals of thought—what will satisfy our needs. Never assume that you know everything or that you have forgotten about or overlooked any subject or task. If you do, it may stop the answer or lesson that you really require to grow.

Looking for results by changing lifestyle is a temporary fix. We are often taught who we are not, but this is society's responsibility. Meditation is to begin to know who we truly are and what we need to know to understand this.

Truth in Life and Meditation

Any curiosity that appears to have little intellectual value at first experience will be like a bud from a garden—who knows what is inside this bud till it blooms?

How does my expression of truth fit into this bud when it begins to open? By becoming the flower or at least by understanding and accepting it.

All that we know is that it comes from the garden and must fit the laws that the garden is made of—in the image of God. To guard our thoughts in such a way so as to prevent them from being abused by others is one thing. To open our thoughts in meditation is quite another—because there are no right or wrong answers—there are only directions to explore. This is why the triangle and the square are used. The sphere makes everything possible—it is consciousness and self-awareness on our plane of measurable energy.

Balance

You cannot eliminate thought because we are immersed in energy that creates thought on all levels. However, we can redirect it to whatever we need or require. There is a need to maintain balance because of our natures and who we are.

A new door is always opening for us—as well as doors now open for exploration and past doors that you may consider to be complete and useful. Allow the heart to speak to you on all matters because the door is your portal, so reenter or enter for the first time with an open mind.

Traps for Meditation

Two men can walk into a pristine forest and one man may see nature at its most beautiful and the other may see a shopping center.

Men who get knocked down do not become angry because of being knocked down, but because of their inability to get back up. Is this the cause of their anger?

It is not in a man to dislike others for what they have accomplished—but only for what they cannot accomplish themselves. Therefore, meditation becomes the direction that develops into the necessary answer.

The dictator does not start out with evil thoughts—only incomplete and badly designed approaches that produce incorrect conclusions within the fabric of his design. This usually creates evil acts to protect his creation when things go wrong. While his friends and guardians take full advantage of its weaknesses for personal gain. This leaves the intended recipients of this project out in the cold with nothing to improve their quality of life.

I must get you to key in on the concepts of each chapter and not on the intellectual drama; this is the reason why a lot of it is written with short statements instead of long stories.

Building Your Coat Of Arms within the Garden

So, how do we learn with intellectual limitations and limited awareness of experience and what is the point?

If you pass by a traveler of the spirit, you have been introduced to another aspect of God. Thank the day for what it is and never forget the essence of the experience—God may have more to demonstrate to you one day.

The virtues that display the moral purposes of life are sown, grown, and cared for in other parts of our garden. Connecting with these will sometimes suggest different colors of emotion—so beware. As a bee goes from flower to flower, gathering nectar to eventually make honey, so we must do the same with life and its experiences to create and display in our tapestry. It is our responsibility to weave them into one tapestry that is hung in your soul, so they all play your song in perfect harmony. This centerpiece of your garden brings all knowledge of virtue together as if it was a centerpiece in a village square. This becomes who we are—a bouquet of life—our names forever.

We share our thoughts with one another. Only if principles of morality are retained and our intentions are virtuous to allow our minds to eliminate anything that is of no value or egocentric, can we then switch over to the portal of wisdom to continue to build our name. (See Ref. A.2.)

When the conversation takes on an aura of wisdom, it can lead to a meditative experience that can ignore all other immoral directions and include virtuous conclusions to the conversation. Ego is an attribute of mind for building purposes that may become a virtuous attribute of self, if you choose to do so. How will you know whether the conversation is moral and virtuous? Listen to your heart. If nothing positive reflects from within, it might be to your advantage to stay away.

Quantum

For this, you need the freedom to travel and, to do this, use these instructions. I hope that you use them often. This symbol has twelve chapters to be used as fuel. This symbol has twelve major components

One is the pilot's counsel and control room.

Two is one line forming the green circle, which is your awareness.

Three through six are the mainframe and guides.

Seven through twelve are the power systems of thinking and use the twelve chapters of cosmic energy.

While practicing your meditations, here are some suggested subjects:

- A Study of the Heart Guiding Our Choices
- Random Thoughts and Understanding of Them

- The Promise as Spiritual Instruction
- The Absolutes the Soul's Window
- The Journey That I Am Compelled To Make
- Images of God As I Know It
- The Simplicity of Virtue, the Habits of a Spiritual Thought
- The Challenge of Adversity
- Freedom and its Direction
- The Gift Our Best Intentions
- Structure of the Paved Road
- Meditations a Portal

During your first experience, you will gain great confidence with your information and experience. This becomes the real faith and belief in God's design as spoken about "ye of little faith." How else could you have faith if you do not have any experience to support faith?

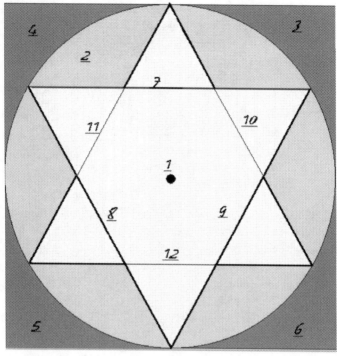

Marked as (A.1)

In the twelve chapters suggested for meditative study there is much writing about how they relate to one another, in order to bypass wishful or exaggerated thinking. These exaggerated thoughts do not provide a correct platform for meditative moral thinking, these thoughts may not be harmful, but they might not be suitable for answers that are supportive to a higher plane of awareness, that would support your needs of spiritual growth. Free will cannot be interfered with to answer a question—only questions that can be answered to elevate your awareness will be answered.

Spiritual Growth Is an Axiom of Creation

All axioms can be demonstrated, but not taught intellectually. Karma represents an accumulation as a critical mass that develops in all things. Growth by meditation is all-inclusive in awareness.

Something very bright, colorful, and intense in its presentation with noticeable changes in energy presentation is one form of mystical experience. There is also a total understanding of a message being conveyed, "All the world is a stage and we are but players on it." I was made aware of this statement and given a whole new perspective of it. The presentation opened up my awareness beyond a picture of a play being performed on a stage. The dynamic energy became alive and filled my mind.

As this developed and very quickly filled my consciousness, I was shown how personalities fit and how they become comfortable. Eventually, they incarnate to a slower measurable static plane that makes up the life and consciousness that we endure. This is how we learn—with the measurable energy that we are submersed in—and it's what we identify as consciousness.

When this intensity diminished, I was left with only a static intellectual awareness. A waning dynamic power lingered for a short while thereafter.

I know that it added something to my awareness as a moment of clarity. As an elevated view of life, from this point on my writing changed to what it is now.

This is the proverbial carrot dangling in front of the donkey. We make fun of dumb animals, but we do the same thing in a spiritual sense.

Look at how children must adjust to living. Some do very well, while others have a difficult time. This is not a punishment, but a learning process. With this we are our brother's keeper to help make these experiences as painless and pleasant as possible; this is also one of society's passions along with man's resistance to change.

Then how does God's wrath fit into all of this—if God is all love?

God's wrath is the laws of creation that constantly rebalance and realign themselves according to their intended design of regeneration. This includes the measurable planes of the cosmos as well as the immeasurable energies called virtue, which point to the direction and growth of society as well as self.

This wrath is also a way for the general population to maintain control and direction as individuals in society. In a nutshell, there are many scary stories of those doing the controlling and those who will be controlled by them.

The ones to be controlled are in hiding—they are the ones who have listened and convinced themselves that they are wrong and this is their fate. They hide and hope that God's wrath will overlook them—this becomes the song of their life. There are a few lone wolves, who drum a different beat for those who need to listen to it.

You know that if you were a doctor, you would have had patients who failed to follow your treatment instructions. Out of desperation and frustration, you might have given them another set of instructions saying, "This may be the last time that I can treat you because you just don't listen to what I am saying. If I hear that your condition has worsened, I will know that this was my last attempt at curing you. Once again, you failed to follow the proper instructions and I am out of options. I cannot reverse your condition. Either you do as I say or you find another doctor. I can no longer be responsible. Get the picture?"

Now you're talking their language—the language of fear.

When reading someone else's experience, do not try to make it your own, just enjoy his or her experience. Look for your very own experience while meditating and follow the rules of interpretation found in these pages. Ego, self-centeredness, and misuse of intellectual expression will be far less capable of becoming part of your experience.

There are two ways to approach living.

The first is to follow all the rules and be saved from the wrath of your shortcomings.

The second is to outgrow them and be free, the spiritual way.

Every place we turn, we are confronted with limitations of one sort or another. No matter how great and free we may think that we are—there are always limitations or consequences. This is the plane of measurement—the third dimension.

Chapter 6

Choose the Direction of Freedom

✦

Freedom can be connected with physical travel—or in using our imaginations in whatever we do. I may choose to be free within the limitations I set for myself. However, freedom must be a choice to grow—not a choice of limitations.

I may choose to take my awareness to new planes in my meditations. By not subjecting myself to social or physical limitations that I am now familiar with; only then will I soar as an eagle or a hawk—always searching for the new and the exiting adventure within me.

Then—and only then—can I follow the paths to travel that this letter instructs me to.

The Beginning Steps

I know who I am—but what will I become in this land that measures everything?

How will I prepare for this adventure of living that may include one or all of these experiences in my life? How will I remain free to who I truly am and become a little wiser for these experiences? For wisdom to be complete and useful it cannot compromise our rational assumptions of these experiences, they must compliment wisdom.

- The Vulnerable
- The Fool
- The Hunter
- The Hunted
- The Wise

My choices in life will always complement my present awareness of self. It will be of value to me as a direction to grow free and wise. For I may choose to compare them with others who have also chosen, their choices may be vastly different from mine. And their choices may spark a sense of curiosity and adventure.

Here is where wisdom will take a stand as your guardian, it will present its guidance if not interfered with. How do I choose—or is choice only a perception that satisfies a need of motion? Motion is the engine of design that can lead us to all that belongs to us.

I must start on any given day—my very best day may very well be someone else's worst day. This is not to say that we are aware of it or had anything to do with it. It is just the beginning of another day.

For me, I say isn't it just the most beautiful day that I have ever seen in my life? What new things will I be made aware of? What old things under the sun will I call new? Who may I give help to?

The Catalyst of Change

What do I really need to know outside my own ignorance? Isn't it just a beautiful day? My own ignorance will get me through the day—until my day is woven with friendships of all sorts. The ones that I call acquaintances, friends, and, most of all, my enemies will teach me what I need to know—even if it is only man's inhumanity.

In my ignorance, they present themselves to remind me that all things are temporary—as well as our beloved ignorance.

When a new day is acknowledged, remember that pain is also temporary. Constant change is our only guarantee. The lessons learned expand our spiritual enlightenment and change weaves your day.

Now then, isn't this the most beautiful day that you have ever seen?

Balance or Defeat

This excitement makes me anxious to reminisce about my experiences by exploring the waves of thought that rush my memory over my triumph. I recall all the disappointments and pain that have overwhelmed me. There were many times that I wanted to concede to defeat.

However, now I will simply relax and thank God. I will walk along some inviting seashore, enjoying the breeze, the smells, and the skyline on the water. We were born and conceived in water—this is our rebirth. If only for a moment, our souls rejoice with a surge of energy from within. Our balance is to worship both the mundane and the infinite within our thinking.

This moment is ours to enjoy—it is God's gift for a job well done. This is all we can know for now—a reflection of self to reminisce on this day.

Virtue is nature and God being the creator of virtue has made every experience a facet of virtue. Free will dictates that we must look for its presentation to us. This presentation is in God's time—not ours. Patience is another facet of virtue.

If balance is associated as a working part of freedom, then trust is a part of its platform and the platform has four sides.

If we truly are explorers, then trust in direction taken must be part of the platform.

Direction is not static. It is motion of all sorts that we are surrounded with—just as the sea is. This motion is energy that is directed from within—it is the engine of growth and balance. (See Ref. A.1.)

Freedom—The Story of Choice

On a bright sunny day, I went to the sea and all I could see was a reflection of me.

My sails are the power of love, selflessness, honesty, and purity to catch the wind. For now, I must move along—knowing full well that someone out there had a far better day than I did. Knowing this should prepare me for almost any situation. With God's blessing, the impossible slowly becomes possible.

Now that I have traveled the seas going from port to port, looking forward to my next experience, I lower the sails of my ship and give my captain his orders. There are new directions that the master within wishes to begin. Mind your instructions given at sleep and inspired by day. Today I will travel the desert and go from oasis to oasis.

I went to the desert with a magic carpet woven of love, purity, selflessness, and honesty. Its corners were secured with bindings called East, West, North, and South. Its direction was set for its woven pattern in the carpet of virtue.

The captain is in firm control with orders in hand to search all directions for the fabled bottles that genies are kept in—not unlike the gods of the seas and skies that have had their adventures as well. Upon sailing into a harbor to moor my ship, I will then travel to my oasis. I am now prepared to identify a new quest.

There will be challenges of awareness and mind. The physical is limited and static in expression, but the soul with personality—in constant growth and masterful expression at times permitted—is the true adventure.

This journey is not for the faint of heart. If there is no wind in the sails of your ship and you run low on safe water, would you drink the seawater? The same goes for the deserts—if you run low on water; would you eat the desert sand out of desperation to satisfy your needs?

My captain must be able to identify the true challenges and their problems of mind. By using the absolutes as his compass, he will set the direction to be taken. Within the designs of God and the language of soul are symbols called the circle, triangle, and square, set the conversation in God by using these through soul and then throughout the cosmos. This makes the storms that produce the great waves of the sea and the mirages of the desert as distorted emotions of the mind. With this information, you can be free—no matter where you are or where you need to go. Keep this in mind and do not overlook its foundation of earth, wind, and water. Fire is the soul—with eternal infinite capacity to transform all energies from the finite to the infinite and back again.

All of these energies must pass through our consciousness while we are awake. Sometimes they are placed within our permanent memories for future use while we are asleep. These variations of energy can be the difference by comparison of a movie, song, poem, or life experience.

Only when we are vulnerable to a revelation can it be called enlightenment—a mystical experience. Remember that these lessons are yours—your expression of them becomes your responsibility—not God's.

All of these things are less than you are. (See Ref. A.1.)

All of these experiences can be separate and unique experiences—from day to day, month to month, and eon to eon. They create a unique personality. Free will becomes the canvas for paints and brushes to create your universe.

The Conclusion

What about the opening statement of freedom—the very reason for this letter? "The reflection of me" is all there is of my consciousness—unless an outside event is permitted to alter it. I use the virtue that I assign to each side of the mystical square as guides for thought and directions for the heart to follow in an infinite sea of energy while I am in a meditative state. (See Ref. A.1.)

A change in my reflection would be brought about by a tear in the fabric of the shade that prevents different and brighter light from penetrating the window. Most of the time these are an actual visual, audio, or sensory experience causing changes in awareness. There is one more experience and this experience grows from the inside out. This experience is from the garden of the soul and knows no fear. The flowers in it have beauty and symmetry. If they are ignored, they will bloom again—these things will make us vulnerable to change from the direction that all virtue emanates. All growth is part of the grand design and cannot be ignored—it is "progress and not perfection."

You have far more strength and power than the boogiemen in your mind. They are only the remnants of your ignorance—treat them as such.

The above experiences can, in one way or another, become the catalyst that changes your perception of awareness and grace. With this I bid you freedom. Remember to never give up and never quit.

Chapter 7

The Challenge of Adversity

✦

Here Then Is the Song of Adversity

Peace is freedom from misfortune. The concept that all things that are different from a designed plan is an unfortunate mishap. It may only be the process of growth to achieve a direction not yet explored and the arrival to a destination totally unimagined and completely unknown.

The Door to Contentment

Contentment is the virtue to bridge adversity. Contentment is the language of the heart. It does not need intellect—only direction from the garden of your soul. This will permit you to know new experiences more completely—provided your approach was above reproach in thought.

Contentment becomes our open door to growth—just as water brings nourishment to allow a flower to bloom. Since contentment is a virtue, it is a cosmic law and is immutable. Contentment is the bridge that will allow a river of adversity to be crossed and not become an impenetrable barrier.

Contentment is the road to acceptance and all that it has to offer.

(Chinese philosophy) the two fundamental principles, one negative, dark, passive, cold, wet, and feminine (yin) and the other (yang) positive, bright, active, dry, hot and masculine. The interactions and balance of these forces in people and nature influence their behavior and fate. *[RHUD]*

A Spiritual Road Map

The Advantages of Acceptance

This becomes an engine with unlimited fuel for the master within to use in meditation and in times of rest. This new fuel adds to the permanent memory of your personality. It will begin to be displayed and be used as you would display and use tools that you already posses and use to accomplish a needed purpose. These tools will become yours for all times to own and use in total freedom as the captain of your ship.

From time to time, the waves of adversity will create joy, anger, fear, guilt, and sorrow. Be careful because these can become emotional addictions—just like the physical addictions.

However, no energy is static and consciousness is a creative potential of mind, which is the birth of emotion.

Contentment opens the door for acceptance and, at the same time, makes the language of contentment far more beautiful than ever before.

Use the Formulas

Mastering adversity is to accept peace. It is directed by contentment and the acceptance of outcomes on the level that you have been made aware. Symbols are the direction of the cosmic. Here are a few examples of direction. (See Ref. 3.2, A.1–12, 3.1.)

Just as nature teaches science what works or does not, always demonstrating the answer in a critical position of exploration to demonstrate the relationship of all things with the timeliness of this answer.

Most of these formulated directions are achieved through the use of intellect. However, intellect will only maintain its level given to it at the time of discovery.

Intellect cannot grow in its intent or status of thought. Intellect is a tool of mind and it has no life of its own—except what we give it.

Provided that you have sufficiently explored the question as mentioned in contentment, free will is never violated and there are no conditions of acceptance placed upon the question. There will always be an answer waiting to be given to you at the proper time. (See Ref. A.1–9.)

The answer may be given immediately and then ignored by us—simply because we have not yet grown into the awareness that we need to be able to see. For this reason, answers may not be made known immediately. But a bridge for the mind will be given for support of your needs by God until, in God's time, you can support your own needs and directions to be traveled.

Chapter 8

The Promise as Spiritual Instructions

✦

In here is a promise that your well - being is yours to keep, especially when things become difficult. I know that this may not seem like much, but it is just a reminder that you are never alone and never left without direction, the answer will change for you according to your surroundings on all levels of active consciousness.

The Initiation with Prayer

The first step is a prayer of need. The mind becomes your road to enter the master's dwelling, which is carefully guarded by your prayer. The prayer becomes the keys. The master of the dwelling may not appear upon entering, but he will leave instructions for you in the entranceway. If you follow them, you will not become lost.

Understanding virtue is incomplete within our awareness. It only shows itself in our necessary expressions to experience our creativity.

As we initiate the thought processes of belief or disbelief, we may set up barriers to the flow of cosmic design and prevent spiritual growth. Bring your complete self. Fear has no place here. Fear will alter truth and limit growth. Bring the keys called prayer with you and you may enter the master's dwelling. A flood of imaginative thinking may not have any more meaning than one word in your thinking that will uniquely describe your need in crises. Look and enjoy all of them. We were given the formulas to guide thought, but we must use them.

Our creativity is an expression of talent required by our needs. These needs can also have a birth by the joining of two or more people. Finally, when growth is beginning to be realized, wisdom must accompany this growth in order for it to be of any positive value.

Diversity as individuals can be created by our many genetic variations along with our God given talents; these two attributes of mind and body that we are born with and because of our social natures is eagerly shared with others in our social settings. A cage of protection is sometimes a welcome mask that becomes a created illusion because of fear—neither has a place here.

The Practical Use of Consciousness

Visualize being open to all virtuous thinking that allows us to be like the sands of the sea. It will allow answers and realities to wash through our consciousness. However, if we are like rock and clay, the water has no depth and we are left alone with our thinking with little nourishment for growth.

Nevertheless, this is the design and support that infinity is capable of giving with total freedom. It is true love and still allows total free will.

In some circles, the moral, the spiritual, and the mystical are all the same. This letter explains my fellowship and permission to study all of this subject matter from within this circle and how they fit together as one. This experience through meditation is a privilege not to be taken lightly.

All experiences that are a part of spiritual growth become limitations to those things that we have outgrown, we will leave them behind on our journey to freedom.

Rock and clay are designed to be building materials, as sand filters and collects debris. Sand can be made into rock. Rock can be ground into sand and clay and then can be made fertile. All things remain in a constant state of change and are beginning or ending a cycle designed in God's time. This is the motion within all growth.

God's Grace of Protection

While becoming friends with a person, you could not help but notice that—like injured birds—they are not free to fly. A wing had become injured. They designed and constructed a cage to protect the wing from being injured any more then what it already has been.

If asked, God can help to mend their wings. Once you are free, you will possess the memory of your free flight and never to be able to recall the cage that kept you in this illusion of safety. This is God's grace and love for us.

"Progress, not perfection" is a spiritual lifestyle that will perpetuate the "never-ending story" and there will be many new chapters to unfold for you.

Some of us require greater help than others do—those who somehow lose their way just have to be reminded.

My Life of Inspiration

The soul allows awareness in the form of direction. This is called inspiration. We do not possess the awareness of virtue in a completed form only what we are accustomed to in our thoughts—even though virtue surrounds us. Although virtue as morality is intended to flow through us, we must learn to permit this condition of flow to exist for all circumstances that we are made familiar with socially, we can redirect this flow to go around us as our chosen direction through our created thoughts of desired directions as free agents of the cosmos.

The Reason for an Explanation

One Saturday afternoon, I found myself sitting alone at my favorite bar. I had told myself many times that I was here for fun and conversation, but I was sitting alone. At that moment, there was a mind-filling explanation with its own energy displayed separately from my own. It was as if I was listening to a conversation with a friend sitting next to me and explaining my purpose of the contract made in the realm of God. As I began to understand this experience within myself, the conversation went something like this.

Before my first breath taken I said to my counterpart that spiritual part of me that upon my last breath I would return once again, I would bring back a bouquet of life greater than anything that I had ever grown and cultivated in God's garden. Maybe there was a remembrance of this contract when first born, but I assure you that the color, sound, touch and developing thoughts of life caused this promise to be forgotten, if not temporarily set aside. Until, conscience began to show me all the weeds in my garden along with this story mentioned above.

What could I do?

I also know and understand through my experiences in prayer and meditation that intelligent life does not end at our last breath and is very active before the first breath. It is the plane of consciousness that we find ourselves on that can be confusing and obscure; but before we take our first breath as humane beings, there are contracts made with God as to our reason for being here as a living breathing entity. How we achieve these commitments in our contract is our free choice as free - thinking people on this earth plane. This is one of my experiences.

The Need to Develop a Dialogue

I have failed to complete this contract—so I asked God, how will I be able to make this up? With no solution or answer, one night a conversation developed in a dream that I had. In my dream, I found myself approaching someone in a flowing white gown. It came to mind that this was the one that I could set things straight with as far as answers for my questions were concerned, this is what my dream had suggested to me - this entity was the same spiritual counterpart, the one the promise was made to before my first breath. So I quickly offered this personality what I had considered the remainder of this promised bouquet along with an apology as to how I had failed.

However, before I could begin my apology, it was touched by this personality that I had approached and the bouquet turned to dust. The seeds from this failed gift were freed and fell to the ground in our presence.

To my surprise, red roses began growing in this space from the many seeds that lay at our feet. The personality exclaimed, "Quickly let us show the master your very beautiful garden with all of its red roses."

It took the better part of four years to begin to understand the real purpose and meaning of this experience. I had to grow into this experience to become aware of its full spiritual and social meaning.

Approximately ten years later in a meditative state in church, I was allowed to listen to still another conversation. I was not in control of the conversation, but I was aware of every word.

Here is the conversation.

The one to speak and control most of the conversation said, "You there, give an accounting of yourself."

In the furthest corner of my mind, I noticed a ragged, scruffy, beaten-up character beginning to stir and stand straight and erect.

The challenger demanded, "Give an accounting of yourself. Where did you go to ask a question of your needs?"

The scruffy character answered without hesitation. Immediately after this answer, he stated, "Welcome. You may enter and study."

With this statement, the two personalities became one and there was a great peace within me. This experience was remembered, but little else. After another ten years, I began to notice an inner growth that had not been there before.

I do not know how much of each conversation and experience was real and how much was symbolic. But, I do know that they were directed toward my consciousness—and consciousness is the prime mover of life. I was permitted to participate and experience a bird's-eye view of how things work. I am still only what life has made me—with all of its challenges and opportunities to grow. I am ever mindful that the good, bad, complete, or incomplete will not appear— unless I try and am successful or fail at the spiritual plans that are given to me.

I have come to the very real conclusion that it is all of our jobs to keep each other as safe and steady as circumstances and abilities permit. This is not always possible, but we must try.

Chapter 9

A Study of the Heart Guiding Our Choices

✦

The Preface to Establish an Example

Sometimes in a meditation exercise, there is what might be looked at as a random thought. However, only after exploring this thought with an open mind and a willingness to learn more on God's terms will there be something new to explore in your meditation.

The Question Given In Meditation

The nature of this thought begins to take a turn of meaning that makes the obscure obvious. A statement was given during a meditation exercise to measure the immeasurable. "There are many people who cling to the only things that they have, while there are others who search for truth. So then, what is evil?"

The statement—as a complete thought—was understandable only as a person's possible attempts at exploring today for the sake of today. It was not measurable as far as any interpretation of incorrect morality.

To Tell of One Person's Story Using Direction Given through the Heart

Let us assume that a choice is somehow presented to challenge a need for a new path to be explored. This moment has been permitted to slip away and only that which remains unchanged is still being clung to.

Because of this inaction, the heart—the communicator of mind and soul—cannot acknowledge and uplift spiritually what might have been a breath of fresh air. It stays gray and dismal. Someone—or something—must be blamed to justify this absence of positive energy. The blame permits us to cling to all that was inadequate and allows the original need for change to be set aside.

The Results of This Decision

The lack of change can be redirected to find a new reason for inaction or wrong action. It becomes an evil act because it detracts from our original destination that we inherited at birth. Perhaps it develops a false testimony that blames others for their inhumanity toward our lifestyle and interferes with our contract with God. Only we know of the contract and are responsible to complete it.

Trauma may be the only path to enlighten the awareness of the individual as to the direction forgotten about—as negative karma.

Openings for another Opportunity

Time is not a factor concerning the infinite love of God—only the right season for replanting new thoughts can restore the journey, this is required to support free will on every level of thought. This is God's grace and love, interference is not a supporting attribute of free will.

The laws of the material world can be an unlimited creative force within higher planes of awareness that we may tap into with prayer and meditation.

As a gardener cultivates his garden, mind functions as a tool to cultivate its soul. The beauty of the garden radiates its diversity as color and form—a hallmark of the gardener's work.

As our awareness becomes focused, so does our ability to understand virtue without limitations. Today, we may find ourselves at the end of the spectrum called awareness. Tomorrow, something new may grow beyond this spectrum. Our responsibility is to experience virtue's use and how it improves our understanding of the cosmos, our use of diversity allows use to understand its results in all of our experiences —this is progress not perfection.

A Vision in Meditation

In a meditation of birds, I followed this as an experience of mind. It was not an observation of the senses; but it could have similar results as an observation. The purpose for giving the example of the birds, lay within the experience of the story—not the story itself.

Follow Through and Grow

Standing and looking at a horizon, I saw a dark line. I noticed some motion and began to see details develop within the line. Slowly I heard some noise and then greater detail and motion. When the noise grew louder and the silhouette outline came closer in this meditation the birds were identified and my attention was drawn to their majesty, beauty, and grace as they passed overhead.

I could have ignored them or continued to be caught up in their passing. As with many thoughts and visions, if we allow our attention to be redirected, the moment will pass us by.

Seize the moment—follow the birds of our thoughts, identify them with clarity, and fly away with them with no restrictions attached to your vision.

People cling to the only thing that they have. The bird story has obvious familiarity, but that may not be the reason for how it was expressed. Unless we clear our minds of assumed conclusions and keep the moment uncontaminated with conclusions directed by intellect, we may miss the intended lesson. For all lessons—whether they are like the bird example or not—teach on many different levels.

We may not be ready for the answer today because all statements are given to us in God's time, not ours.

A journey as an adventure of the heart is a never-ending story. Look back only to get better direction for the future—the rest will take care of itself.

The Meditation

The fire of consciousness is the language of the heart. It reminds you to look beyond what you may consider to be an answer to a thought, circumstance, or question. However, it does not express itself through intellectual means. Emotion can alter the very meaning of something presented in an intellectual form, but the heart will stand firm at odds with your intellect—unchanged in its convictions.

The opposing forces of nature equal awareness. People cling to things because they have nothing else—addictions of all kinds are symptoms that attract attention to this lifestyle.

Does this mean then that they may be unwilling to acknowledge anything else? Truth is not an answer, but a new direction to develop a new awareness. We must be willing to leave the old to embrace the new.

The message of the birds may be that new direction. Each of us may see something different in this meditation because of what we need for growth. The message is a living message and has many facets to it. Some facets we already understand and some will be revealed. As we grow into the full meaning of this message later in our spiritual development, the introduction will be remembered and reveal facets from the past. Depth and beauty of design are God's rewards for our diligence and persistence.

If growth is consciously noticed, it is a proven endorsement of following God's design. It can only be an endorsement if the heart approves of the garden that now grows and bears fruit with all of its delightful aromas, exciting colors, and patterns of design. The mind of self is as the opening buds of roses and other flowers in the garden. A weakness or defect of character ceases to be a weakness when its true nature is permitted to develop into full bloom in your garden.

The very nature of a defect is to show us our limitations. Triumphs are one with God and do not show themselves in any other way—except with morality and discipleship of virtue.

But what is virtue?

It is certainly not an opinion of anything and it is not a social event. In your meditations, the pictures that develop in your mind can be expressed in words, music, painting, sculpture, or in our relationships with others.

This is as close as we can come to knowing what virtue is—a feeling of freedom in spiritual expression along the path called truth.

In Conclusion

Evil cannot be our struggle to be free—only our refusal to grow from within and walk the walk as an expression of such.

To experience a complete thought in meditation and then analyze it with intellect and making it the important aspect of the experience, we lose the integrity of the experience. Total understanding of awareness is our goal.

Writing these letters to others eliminates the interference of self by getting outside of one's self. This exercise allows the mind to explore and express itself, using the cosmic as its book and taking anyone from beginning to end of each one's center of being. This is where your real workshop waits for your involvement—not one's own opinions as a tool.

As mind resonates with soul through its adventures of life, the notes of sound become music, color becomes art, and poetry wraps around life.

When the mind touches another aspect of soul, growth continues and enlightens. This allows true freedom to become the gift of giving and the experience of sharing these gifts. This continued growth is a new expression of life that may not have been there yesterday.

Always choose a lifestyle that will fertilize your garden of mind, so you as the gardener will reap the harvest in the fall of your life.

If your thinking is thoughtless, self-centered, less than virtuous, or interferes with free will, you will have less impact within the scheme of things. Negative destructive thoughts do not flow through the cosmos—they are retained within the sphere of your own consciousness and limited to your own power and strength. (See Ref. Chap A, plate A.1, A.2, A.3, A.4.)

When the sphere, triangle, and square are compromised with irrational thinking and their purpose of design ignored, it is a developed type of self-destruction at worst—or irrational thinking at best.

This is the design of the cosmos—just as pain is designed into our physical third-dimensional existence. There is a spiritual pain as well in the fourth dimension that shows in our actions and expressions in the third dimension.

We misuse both of them.

Chapter 10

The Journey I Am Compelled To Make

✦

This letter is to give your journey more freedom than what you might have thought possible. Upon the conception of a desired destination—which can be launched in one's mind by the tools we call imagination and intellect—some journeys become a dream and others become lifestyle experiences.

Imagination is the sum total of all our experiences of mind and soul personality. Permanent memory and talent are a mixture designed and maintained by the soul's need to grow in respect to God's love. Life's beginnings lend themselves to past, present, and future highways of an incomplete destination. The instructions for this journey are in talent and intellect. Intellect is a taught outer expression of self. Talent displays itself—waiting for you to use it.

Also when embarking on a journey, if at all possible be careful not to limit your journey to past, present, or future tense.

My Corner of the World

My corner of the world is my gift to myself. Everything in my corner of the world is absolutely perfect. I could not ask for anything more—except for a few minor things. The garden in my world is beginning to become unsettling. The food does not appear to satisfy my nutritional needs and the drinking fountains no longer quench my thirst as they once did.

I must leave my corner of the world to add something to my creation. However, I am not sure what this addition would be. I must go on a journey and search for a solution.

The Road Traveled

As I travel my road, some things are familiar. Other things that I come to notice beckon for no reason, but attract. I must slow down.

Then I say I know you—but from where? Maybe I will stop and stay for a while since there is time on this journey to do so. It is on the road that I travel, but I do not claim it as mine. I must stop for a while and when I leave, know that it was never mine—and never will be. Or will it?

My decisions made out of curiosity will make this journey more complete than before this road was taken. Any thought that can be measured is also limited in its scope. When an answer comes to you by other means than intellectual reason, it may not fit your present needs and requests in prayer, but point to a more spiritual expression—unlike anything that you expected.

Who could I ask a question while I am exploring? Who knows my journey well enough for me to be able to ask? How then do I trust?

The Absolutes

Upon the conception of your thoughts, wisdom must satisfy the design of the square. These things are a part of the law of proportion and with this assurance to myself, I am sure that my world is perfect. And I am sure that anyone could see how well adjusted it is—all I need are a few minor adjustments. Isn't this the way we all start a journey, with the complete assurance to ourselves that our understanding is above reproach and there will be little for us to learn.

Learning To Trust Your Search

Whether it is in our daily lives, in the quiet of the day, or in an evening meditation, there is always a journey to complete. How shall I set my direction to know that I will receive the correct answer for proper guidance? I must start by seeking the God of my understanding so that my journey is in my best interest and I can trust what has been revealed. Recognize your freedom—whether you are asking a question or engaging in conversation with God, worthy masters, saints, sages or religious leaders.

The more open minded and honest my approach, the less likely I am to become "the will-o'-the wisp." (See Ref. Folklore.)

Friendships can be one way of suggesting trust. However, some friendships are of convenience and others will last for all time. This distinction involving friendships is important when your spiritual well being is at risk or you are recognizing that something new is to be learned through our prayers and meditations.

Searching within the descriptions of entities throughout the cosmos—they are active or inactive.

The Active Personality

Active personalities are permitted to keep their total and complete personalities—this gives them free will outside of their own sphere of consciousness. This awareness is exactly what we experience—with limited expression—on this third-dimensional plane as consciousness. Occasionally we can experience the consciousness on a higher plane while maintaining our own consciousness. This is not easy and is only done very selectively. This as a gift is earned through God's love for certain entities whose compliance with the design of virtue and their understanding of moral use with the energies of the cosmos. These personalities will always assist in helping other personalities develop and grow as free, talented, and unique individuals—without interfering with their free will. This is permitted by having all of the energies of the cosmos at their disposal to assist in your spiritual growth and consciousness.

Nothing less than this could—or would—be considered. There is value placed on correct action and not on inaction. Delaying a decision until a more favorable time fails to become the correct time and therefore may never be acted upon. Tennyson said, "It is better to have loved and lost than to have never loved at all." They will do everything in their power to help you—without interfering with your free choice or agreed-upon experiences. These experiences may be referred to as your karma or lessons. Their nature does not interfere, but helps and maintains their contract with God as free entities. Freedom is all that there is and choice is a part of God's virtue.

The Inactive Personality

The inactive personality is not permitted to operate freely outside its own universe of awareness. This may be due to the fact that they have not yet acquired the proper experience to earn the right and trust of this freedom of expression. However, there are others who are trapped holding the mundane as more important than the infinite creations within the cosmos. None of these personalities can give you direction or counsel that would be of any benefit to your growth. If anything, some of these personalities would benefit to gain your confidence and then use your freedom as a living breathing person for their own supposed gains—while theirs is still being kept in check. In order not to become part of their thought processes, do not find fault with them—only with their actions that have been taken for incorrect reasons. This ensures that the misuse of your ego will never become involved as an expression of disagreement to conflict with theirs. Their acts should only be addressed in a fashion of their intended purpose, reason, and outcome of their actions, which are to limit and enslave those who may be considering their position within the cosmos. This is their understanding of freedom—an illusion of self-importance and worth.

Breadcrumbs represent things that are mundane, but can be thought of as great spiritual protection or importance as far as direction is concerned. In the story of Hansel and Gretel, the breadcrumbs that they dropped and left as a trail to find their way home were eaten by birds and they lost their way.

What directions have we occasionally lost by a change in interpretation?

What promises have been forgotten as our true missions of accomplishments?

What relationships have resulted in disappointments instead of enduring friendships?

What paralyzing fears have controlled our missions?

Life can cause us to change our focus occasionally. We may lose our way, but nothing is ever permanent—only occasionally painful.

How many facets have we noticed on the cosmic jewel of our own design? How many facets have you discovered so far?

All things that exist are of this nature and are part of what is being built by us on an infinite, unending expanding ocean of virtue.

If it is not virtue, it does not—and cannot—exist.

Giving importance to a mundane question or statement should be kept in mind since everything can be measured and limited in its expression of true need. Your vision may be limited to a mundane reference as an answer—especially if all of your thoughts start with this premise.

Infinity cannot be described intellectually without diminishing its true nature. Unless we are permitted to understand through awareness, it is awkward—if not impossible—to express with words.

So how else can this awareness be expressed?

We will allow our thoughts to parallel infinity as closely as possible and to develop truth as it is seen, felt, or heard at that instant. This will leave growth and change open and waiting for the next contact with uncontested awareness. Following these instructions will give confidence that the answers are true and powerful—and will permit even greater freedom. In this manner, religion and philosophy are for man. God emanates those things that they are made of. Enjoy and share this banquet of life—it is always there and will never end.

Do not try to understand your words or concepts with intellect. Step into them with your consciousness and will for the purpose of meditation.

Picture the triangle pointing up and your awareness of God and all the morality that you can be aware of—then ask your question, seek your direction, and walk with God. Chapter 5, a.1 lines 10, 11, 12 with composite made up of numbers 1&2.

Become Part of the Thought

Your contract with God will match your potential personality and disposition as the tools needed to be complete when your journey ends. It is your responsibility to keep all of this in balance.

There are seven billion people on this earth plane and many more in the cosmic. God knows all of them, but the activity of the inner circle can only work with the ones that have been noticed. These are the ones that become elevated in stature—they have developed talents and attitudes toward the fulfillment of destinies that concern others and their development of life skills.

You have been noticed.

How do I know that this is correct?

These letters have been given to me as a song of life. My greatest concern is that I have picked the correct verbiage and phrases so you will realize the greatest benefit from them in order to celebrate your life.

Chapter 11

Structure of the Paved Road

✦

Structure Is the Realm of Exploration in All Things

Studying through exploring the spiritual is the beginning to knowing God's design. The structure of God's design starts with chaos and develops into unending creativity. Elevate your awareness—guided by the examples in this book and in your life experiences.

The very word structure suggests that something has been erected, but what will this beacon of energy become if it cannot be demonstrated with description? It will become your sanctuary.

Travel and Be Free

Awareness and talent are the beginning of infinite creativity in an environment of unchanging circumstances. Thoughts show direction, while awareness supplies motion to open all doors and the choices they hold. All thoughts must be kept as simple and basic as possible—so as not to compromise direction or maybe to more easily avoid another direction.

If we guard our thoughts as being complete, we refuse to let them grow and develop as unlimited experiences. Due to this choice, the cosmic would be interfering with our free will—this is not permitted and things will become static and unchanging instead of creative.

Your image of God will continue to widen and grow, becoming more and more encompassing in everything that you do and question—within your meditations and accomplishments.

To truly explore God, only positive thoughts will flow through the cosmos. Anything negative will not—for they are man's creation and will remain here.

Spiritual Needs

The picture that becomes us is painted by life; we are the canvas that displays this painting. The artist who chooses the format and color scheme will become the subject and title and will be known as the artist wisdom. Community and friendship will become the tools that paint growth.

A word to describe a thought has its birth within a promise and first breath. Your first breath is your promise as well as your contract of life. The very things that pure gold represent to us in nature—above all other elements—are like virtuous deeds that demonstrate great social value as deeds, this supports your contract of life. The contract of life that we agree to before taking our first breath, is ours to complete using our own perception and talents as we see fit to use them, this is our freedom.

Energy can be altered in appearance—but not eliminated in essence.

The next paragraphs may help keep spiritual needs in a more easily focused position in spite of every day affairs.

Clear and precise thoughts create the most complete picture of communication—a picture is worth a thousand words.

My ability to convey a complete thought with words in spiritual matter is limited. The shades and color that are a part of our spiritual makeup are not a part of our ability to express this awareness.

At the same time, my benefits from writing these pages sharpen and develop awareness to greater clarity and contrast. I hope that this will have similar results as you read, write, and study all spiritual material.

Remember that imagination is the sum total of all our experiences. Where have you been and where are you going?

Creating Wisdom

When I was a younger man, I was not free, but I knew people who were free beyond what I could understand.

As my spiritual awareness grew because of my life experiences, so did the need to address these experiences. I learned that the intellect used in everyday social affairs had great advantages that could be expressed as one statement—in who I am spiritually.

Wisdom is the fruit of failure.

I look back at failure with twenty-twenty hindsight. Failure resides on a new plane of consciousness—where thoughts show direction for talent to explore and create new adventures for the growth of new wisdom to ripen on the vines of life.

Let your structure be like the structure of an iceberg—the top part is exposed for intellectual expression to deal with everyday affairs. However, under the sea, the larger part of the iceberg is the stabilizing anchor—the essence of your soul. Let intellect direct your awareness to the part of self that makes life possible with meaning and direction. Your real power comes from within your structure, the place where everything sought-out is greater than you are.

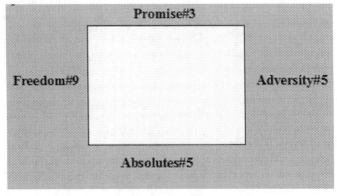

Square—11.1
(labeled promise, freedom, adversity, and absolutes)

The square once more is given to use as God's formula to develop wisdom in your meditations. Spiritual structure seems to develop more completely from the inside out—instead of from experiences of the day. These experiences tend to be much more traumatic—sometimes referred to as the lessons of karma—and are limited to a specific social experience.

The object is to learn from the more peaceful and complete awareness—spiritual experiences. This allows you to pick a more comfortable direction and level of understanding that will give you the optimum experience based on God's teaching and not man's.

These things cannot be kept in mind as a complete understanding—only aspects of them. Only carefully chosen thoughts from the four previous chapters should be chosen and tried. Choose each subject and relate it to the principles of the other three chapters for your meditation.

These basic and simple geometric symbols are portals of awareness within the cosmos. All other geometric forms are man's creation and refer to what man is building or has built.

Eventually you will be able to sit almost anyplace, anytime and follow a picture or sea of thought from one word or concept using the formula of the square or the triangle. However, do not memorize any of this. Just become familiar with it through your inner self, it will guide you. As it expands and develops, you will be surprised at the new horizons shown to you.

The mundane is important, but so is the weather. The weather is the model for the mundane because of its storms of earth, wind, fire, and water.

The storms of society are known as the apocalypse. Its traumas are pestilence, war, disease, and famine. However, to meditate in the direction of the infinite is peaceful, uplifting, and renewing to one's self-awareness. This leaves us open to new adventures and pleasant experiences.

Chapter 12

The Absolutes are the Soul's Window to Wisdom.

✦

While contemplating my meditative experiences, it had become very clear to me that there are no special words to describe the emotional and elevated consciousness that accompany such experiences.

To use the absolutes correctly in your meditations will raise your consciousness to a place beyond where the aurora borealis was born and the planets sing a song of motion in a quiet whisper. This room incubates nebulas and directs its children—called galaxies. Here, the word *universe* is too limiting except for a window that we know as meditation, this window can take us beyond all these above descriptions mentioned. This window is a portal to all of our journeys. All things that have to be accomplished will involve you in what becomes exciting on your roads of travel. Which road is the one that you have chosen first?

Nature of a Formula

The one window that I find the most beautiful comes with:

- Four sides
- Four words
- Four colors
- Four stories

Each side—with its own energy of God to be used as deeds—has its own rewards. However, to pass through the center of this window is to experience a freedom beyond what we know in our daily living with this formula's direction and our experience with using it. The closest example of this feeling might be the observation of some of God's creations in nature; one of them the cuttlefish or the octopus-for both can blend in with their surroundings. With both of these examples, it is the outer cover that changes. For us to remotely relate to this example, it would be your mind and awareness that will more completely blend in with God's virtue. This is as close to as any objective example that I could think of that might match the experience of meditation using the formula known as the Absolutes. The square is just a geometric shape to symbolize a solid base or platform to launch your meditation from your present awareness to an elevated one closer to God's perfection. You too will experience similar adventures of soul and mind directed by your captain. With these four sides, beauty has no limitations. They not only tell their stories in color, song, and vibrant texture, but they begin to reflect and harmonize with one another. They give off an infinite sandbox where imagination and mind can play contentedly. As always, tomorrow will be another day with new adventures to experience.

Because of this window, there will be a growth of wisdom. It will allow a free and elevated awareness to address a question that I need to explore in meditation. I will hold this picture in my mind, turn it over to my higher power in meditation, and pray to seek an awareness of mind that surpasses any intellectual experience as an answer that I have been searching for.

The Meditation

This meditation requires the use of the square - as a balance of thought, when this occurs the window becomes not a formula of thought, but a road to be traveled. Before I begin to meditate, I must establish my current understanding of <u>love</u> as best as I can. This definition must be challenged and tempered by establishing my useful understanding of <u>unselfishness</u>. The freest and purest form of love can only be experienced when accompanied by unselfishness. However, this creates a dilemma of mind; once again "you don't know what you don't know." Therefore, there are two checks of thought and lifestyle to be applied to love and unselfishness. One is <u>purity</u> and the other <u>honesty</u> of intent. This becomes a key to enter my window to everything—the focal point of mind and free, uninhibited consciousness to explore my new directions. This is not only an answer, but it is also growth because all wisdom is virtue and virtue is infinite by its very design. (See Ref. A.2.)

This use of the absolutes is a description of a formula. The mystery of formulas is that once they are discovered and used, they become effortless. All formulas are reflections of the grand design of the cosmos, they repeat with predicted results. However, they must be free of all agenda—only what it is capable of being manifested. The nature of all formulas is that they work only as designed. This formula's name is humility and humility is the direction of wisdom.

Now that I have established a required direction and need, let me establish some examples to explore. The artist uses common themes to display the depths of talent of their abilities:

- Colors of objects
- Shapes and themes
- Paints, sketches, or photography for two-dimensional displaying
- Sculpture with various media for three-dimensional displaying
- Writing—poetry, novels, and manuscripts of all kinds
- Cooking to express culinary talents

These pleasurable experiences inspire us to be moved in our own unique way to mirror these experiences—using our own talents with the media of our choice.

How else could this be accomplished if the formula was not available to our understanding? What if we simply never tried or even gave it a brief consideration? With this spiritual aspect of thought, we can guide proper development and habit of our thinking.

The design of the cosmos uses virtue as its superstructure just as a skyscraper is designed. Altering a skyscraper's I-beams, which support its outer skeleton, inner walls, and stairways, will eventually cause the entire building to collapse. We certainly could not destroy the cosmic in this manner, but we are very capable of destroying ourselves. We were made in God's image—from the smallest particle to the largest component—from microcosm to macrocosm.

When we move through our own universal consciousness, we can create ripples of discord under the proper circumstances. These ripples of inharmonious energy are similar to the winds pushing on our oceans in varying intensities and directions until pressure points build to enormous strengths and create huge destructive waves that are more than one hundred feet high. These rogue waves are responsible for sinking or seriously damaging many large ships—not to mention the smaller ones that have never been found again. As with these waves, we cannot outmaneuver our own negative ripples of mind. However, they can be quieted, subdued, and redirected into positive energy. The formula of humility is one way to accomplish this.

The Balance of Observation

The absolutes—love, unselfishness, purity, and honesty—are capable of reducing subject matter to its simplest and most basic meanings.

These four words used in one teaching most completely describe the essence of virtue in God.

Pick your own four words and establish them in the square, using your four absolutes as the corners. This will help you to better understand your window. By using the four words in this letter to support your window of thought and dream, it will help you understand past relationships and ventures. (See Ref. A.1, 11.1)

Practice these four words or, if you prefer, pick four different words. As long as they are moral, they will bring results to you.

To practice this is to practice proper thinking that will support the amulet. (See Ref. A.1, lines 3–6.)

Notice that the circle of consciousness is an inscribed circle and the square supports all of this as part the amulet. (See Ref. A. 1–2.)

Hold this in mind as completely as possible, direct your question at the base or bottom of the triangle - the triangle with its apex at the highest position - and release it into the cosmos. Be confident that you will receive an answer—provided your question can be answered.

On all other days that could be your very first day of a new adventure, you may find yourself surrounded with water, mountains, or the dessert, or possibly all three. For this day, today it is not mine only the memory of such a day from the past. But, the roads to these memories are familiar to me and so I use them whenever the opportunity knocks on my door. All other days I must build wisdom with my freedom, wisdom is fleeting so I find myself chasing it. It becomes the stewardship of my soul with constant work to keep the weeds of life at bay and my thoughts from becoming old and infertile. But for you here are the roads that are traveled whenever the chance is given.

In closing, remember the very important attribute called imagination. Imagination is greater than all measurable things. Imagination gives color and texture to all virtue that we use and speak of—not only in our daily affairs, but in our memories as well. It is the support for our thoughts in belief and faith. Last but not least, it spearheads and directs all things that are thought to be impossible and makes them possible.

Use your imagination wisely and often and may God bless your efforts.

Yours truly,
Robert

<u>Diminishing Spiral</u>

✦

Traveling the diminishing spiral or that has been known as "The temple of God."

All motion moves in one direction of moral being. Here you are inspired to enter at will as a sanctuary from your toiling consciousness to rest and reside in with your meditations and prayers to communicate your wishes and desires of mind. This becomes your home as you travel up the circular coils, and begin your journey to the top. The alternative to this sanctuary is to weather spiritual pain like Trojans with adopted life styles to help support this pain until we outgrow it or until death should come first.

So then a prayer after emerging yourself within this spiral is, that what ever I approach with one or five of all my senses and that I am willing to ignore will lead me to learn nothing, but I can be momentarily all consumed in this moment and learn everything I need to know for today.

The Structure Relating To Us

A coil is as a component within the makeup of the spiral and is simply this; a coil is a circle that represents completeness, it also represents our consciousness that makes up our awareness.

There is an awareness that belongs to a greater all including sphere, that is far more subtle in thought of purpose known as the soul. Then considering this, all things must be the same in structure except for our unfamiliarity in our journey in life.

Introduction to Travel

As we travel in the direction that is permitted within the spiral, it becomes a direction of moral being and spiritual growth that increases our awareness. This becomes the mechanism that allows us to adjust thoughts in their act of being that are more encompassing in all things, for this is the realm of God.

Each coil of the spiral over laps the other coil in its essence of contents, this is the direction of God; as its lessons repeat themselves on an ever-evolving higher plain of consciousness, this becomes the road that must be traveled.

Inner and Outer Growth

As a spiritual framework grows with age and experience within us and as we explore the spirals that concern our journey spoken of in this letter; this will permit ones expression of a greater spiritual knowledge that has developed within the soul's personality. This expression is added to the attributes of mind as they display the things from the past that will more completely develop and grow an elevated spiritual expression of self.

As our awareness expands within the spiral room and as our lesser thoughts begin to diminish with our approach to the top, there becomes a limitation imposed on the baggage that we are permitted to take on our journey. This leads us to ponder the mysteries within the mystery; as we begin to learn that all things that are part of the third dimension must stay in this third dimension. Only the memories of the past were all this started with no seemingly controllable direction that we are sure belongs to us; these are the instincts and awareness that portray our thoughts and actions in life's quandaries and life styles.

Here eccentricities, addictions, and defects of character show us and become reminders of what we cannot take with us. For lack of a better example, this is like the monkey with a closed fist wrapped around a nut in a jar and unless he lets go of the nut, his closed fist is too large to be removed from the jar's smaller opening. So then, for the monkey to be free he must let go of the nut to be able to remove his hand from the jar.

Our Relationship To Our Growth

The microcosm represents spiritual inner growth and is the test pilot within a limited plane known as the third dimension. Here ego and intellect get us through life, especially in our youth. While maturity of age and experience permit us to look back at what we did correctly or incorrectly surrounded by the support of the soul's gentle encouragements from within its place within the macrocosm. All of this is supported by our attributes of mind that we have further developed in life to complete the journey of the day.

The fuel used on this plane is known as sin and sin is measured with morality, which is all-inclusive in the macrocosm. And is always keeping the scientific, metaphysical, and the philosophical guided with prayer, communion, and confession for these three things are everything to proper direction.

Trying to explain the greater cycle with intellect reverts us back to the smaller cycle, to understand the greater requires our inner awareness.

As we grow in awareness within the microcosm of self, we slowly evolve in spirit and soul of the macrocosm, but at an entirely different rate called the infinite. To more graphically explain this statement I will use something like the cogs or gears of a clock. One will spin very fast with a unit of measure in seconds, hours, days, years, and distances of many descriptions; while the other larger cog driven by the smaller cog will use infinity as its measure. Now ponder the life cycle of the gnat verses the great sea turtle, all things in a cycle of living are relative to its own journey and not necessarily the twenty-four hour day.

Supporting the Design

Here then is the paradox of our understanding, our days are taken up with the smaller cog and its completeness from beginning to end of one life cycle.

As the success or failure of this life cycle is described and understood as "seeds being cast on fertile or barren soil" will become our barometer of life. The experience and spiritual ground that we travel and develop with in our own small cog of awareness is determination and desire. "The chicken or the egg" is a subject that can approach the weak and the strong in determination and inner strength of living; if the chick does not break through the shell of the egg it will die. So it is the relationship of the chicken to the egg that becomes important, not which one of them came first?

Our Final Direction

Concerning the larger cog is the direction of all virtue and some of this virtue is demonstrated as personality traits and life styles that we will need to in part complete the journey of the larger cog and become ready to join a higher plane of spirituality. These can be described as the tapestries of awareness that we slowly sew together and add to our life of experiences, they become part of our whole being of experiences. When this garment is complete in the embrace of God, the garment will fit to display a unique signature that is who we truly are. This does not include our interpretations of virtue based on our limited perceptions of living but a greater understanding.

For while the smaller collective journeys are set aside and only used in our memory to guide us through the greater journey by using our imagination, permanent memory, and our God given talents. The larger cog is where mastership of our being develops and where like the rose in a garden, the pedals of this flower open to show its beauty and uniqueness. All of this made possible because of the chicks work in leaving its eggshell. The angles were put here to guide us as we grow and travel on our journey, each one having its own set of rules to guide us by as our journey continues on. Now what unit of measure should we assign to the greater journey of God's design?

Following the Road Signs

Although there may be suffering, misery, confusion, joy, and happiness, we will make ourselves available to one another in our experiences shared as companions in life on this seemingly endless journey.

So, now what value of measurement should we put on this? It is our renewed curiosity and the promise of greater freedom within God that gives us the willingness to build a new life within the smaller cog and continue our journey to become a greater part of the soul and its personality. There is always the promise of greater reward and understanding on this seemingly unending journey of greater beauty with more complete understanding then what we are shown today.

Our imaginations are always being prodded by our surroundings like the seas and the oceans of the world, the trees and the forests on land, all of them displaying animate and inanimate life forms that we can relate to in God's domain of a spiritual understanding. We must use these experiences as examples to feed on and learn by, for they are the fuel supplied to us for the day.

And as once again a reminder that we are spiritual beings that will grow in the larger plane called infinity where these things cannot go; only the experiences of imagination become the corner stone and hallmark of our journey.

The learned delicate balance through nature that is required to maintain relationship and related design identities help to build the awareness of proportion and continued balance for our own growth to continue our journey.

All of this being encouraged from those who have already made this journey of unending freedom as we are becoming increasingly aware of our true birth place within God.

In the world of measured concepts, the distance between two points is a straight line; while in the spiritual and metaphysical concepts of the shortest distance between two points becomes the seemingly longer way around, for there are no distances to measure only accomplishments. So, in times when we fell incomplete it is only that our journey is not yet over.

Yours truly,
Robert Hrebin